Perfect tips to building a healthy Relationship everyday

Chapter 1

Questions to ask before getting married

You've found the one you want, and you're engaged to be married, but ask yourself this: Are you really prepared for married life? That is the question most "about-to-get- married" couple ask often. I will give you the perfect answer.

Before getting married you must know this

Marriage is a union between a man and a woman, but it is interesting to note that the definition of **a successful marriage** means different things to different people. This is because people's family histories, religious beliefs, and moral standards all play a role in determining what constitutes a successful marriage. Know this that;

By the time you and your partner are serious enough to sign a certificate, you might think you know everything there is to know about each other. Still, we are all different, and there are many things couples should talk about but often don't until long after they've walked down the aisle.

However, **keep this in your heart**; if you ask the right questions before you get married, you'll probably learn about his/her needs, dreams, and expectations for your life together that you hadn't thought about before.

But a lot of couples who want to get engaged don't know what to talk about. Even though your goals and preferences will change over time.

Here are some "pre-engagement questionnaire" that can help you avoid some conflicts in the future. Or, at the very least, the questions will help you figure out how to deal with them together.

"I tell people to have these talks before they get engaged, because it can be hard to leave once you start planning a wedding and you are excited,"

As a relationship counselor, one of my greatest wishes is to be able to work with engaged couples before they tie the knot. The majority of the couples I treat for therapy have issues that have been building up for years when they first come in. People have varied perspectives on marriage, as well as varying ideas and expectations around it.

Here is a list of 25 key things to ask before getting married, according to several experts. These topics range from where you will spend the holidays to how you would divide your finances.

25 key questions to ask before getting married

A lot of "already-married" couple that are not getting what they expected in their marriage can relate to this questionnaire. If you are already married, there is enough time to adjust and make your marriage sweeter. BEFORE GETTING MARRIED; ASK YOURSELF THIS

What is the purpose of my marriage?

"Why get married when there are so many couples in this day and age who choose not to do so? The intensity of our affections for one another should not be the sole consideration in our marital decisions. That means Our strong romantic feelings should not only be the reason why we are getting married "What do you think marriage will bring to the relationship between the two of you? And in terms of the way you live your life as an individual?"

How do you respond when things go in a different direction than you expected?

"Something that a lot of people don't understand coming into marriage is how planned out they have their lives. Some people haven't even figured out their life first before getting married. This is a huge red flag. "It's something that a lot of people don't realize." When something unexpected occurs that throws a wrench into those plans, it may put a strain on the relationship. When thinking about your response, it could be helpful to look back to a prior example.

How do we now manage conflicts with one another? How well do we handle disagreements?

"Is there one among you who is so obstinate that you just can't seem to find a way to compromise? Or are you the kind of person who is so scared of conflicts that you never bring up the things that bother you and run away from confrontation when it arises? These are unhealthy tendencies that need to be addressed before getting married

How much more do you appreciate the time you spend together as opposed to the time you spend apart?

Will one of you anticipate that you will accomplish everything together as a married unit, while the other of you will need a significant amount of time for yourself? I told a couple a long time ago, when two people are dating, they should spend a significant amount of time together. "Once a person gets comfortable into the pattern of being married, a lot of them discover that they miss their freedom, and as a result, they may draw back a little bit."

Is the marriage of your parents a source of motivation for you to get married?

"If that's the case, why? If not, what are the reasons behind that? "Discuss in detail what each of you considers being the hallmarks of a fruitful partnership.

Do you want kids?

It's possible that your responses may change and evolve over time, but it's crucial to revisit this topic right now anyway. "If one person says, '100 percent I want kids,' and the other says, 'I 100% percent don't,' that's probably going to be a no-go moving ahead "That's probably going to be a no-go moving forward."

What happens if we are unable to produce children of our own biologically?

This question has made kept a lot of couple confused. How would you want to handle the difficulties associated with fertility? What happens if there is a spontaneous abortion? And what are your thoughts on having a kid via in vitro fertilization or through adoption?

What do you think the role of children will be in our family?

"I've treated a number of couples, and after they have kids, it sort of takes over the relationship." "One of them is truly yearning for time spent together as a couple, while the other is simply completely preoccupied with the child. That may lead to a significant amount of stress for the pair." That one member of the relationship anticipates having a ladies' night out or guys' night out each and every week is fantastic information to have at this point.

How do you plan to deal with the situation if we start to drift apart?

There will be moments when the "couple" portion of being in a relationship may seem like a distant memory because of the demands of work, children, and life in general. "Who among the group is most likely to raise the alarm? And how exactly do you plan to reconnect?"

How do you plan to deal with the ups and downs of our sexual relationship?

This is a more fruitful question to ask rather than "how frequently will we have sex?" since the frequency of sexual activity will change throughout the course of the relationship. "Sexual pleasure may correspond to relationship satisfaction."so it's crucial that couples be more or less on the same page when it comes to what they want from the sexual portion of their relationship.

If I'm not satisfying your sexual demands, how do you expect them to be satisfied elsewhere?

This may provide an opportunity for you to discuss topics like as masturbation, pornography, or even the concept of consensual non-monogamy, such as an open marriage, and your perspectives on these topics.

What kind of holiday plans do you have in mind for every year?

Is it possible that one of you imagines spending Christmas with your family while the other of you fantasizes about going to Disney World? If you're thinking about getting married, you've probably already reached a decision about how you want to go with your relationship. However, one of you could believe that this decision should be revised once you are married, especially if you have children.

What are your thoughts on vacations, and how often do you see taking them in the future?

If, for example, going on a trip together every year is very important to you, then you should be aware that you and your partner will need to set aside money in the future to cover the cost of doing so.

Do you want to save a lot of money in the beginning of your career, or do you want to save up for things like a trip or a new TV in spurts?

When you get married, one of you could think that you'll be looking for a new home, while the other of you might imagine that you'll be doing more traveling and going out to fancy restaurants.

Do you want to keep your money in separate bank accounts, or would you rather share all of your assets?

The financial arrangement that a married couple comes upon is always unique to their partnership. "A excellent method for a lot of people is to have a joint bank account for costs, "but then designate an amount to put into a personal bank account." In this manner, you can put money aside throughout the year so that you don't have to argue over who gets what when you want to purchase a new toy.

Are we all on the same page on how the work gets done in our house?

The question of who performs the duties and how frequently they are done is a recurrent one for me. She suggests determining early on who would be in charge of household chores including cooking, cleaning, and maintaining the yard. Discuss how you'll manage it when one of you neglects to do a duty that's allocated to you," so you should talk about how you'll handle the situation.

When is it that you feel that I love you the most?

For instance, "when you prepare me lunch" and "when you give me a huge embrace" are both examples of "when you."

How do you express love?

Taking the exam "Love Languages" may help you identify the words to use to describe what you're feeling.

Finish the following sentence: "When my partner _____, I am able to talk about how I am feeling in a way that makes me feel the most at ease.

Think back to a moment when you had to start a difficult discussion, and try to recall what you did that made it easier for you to start talking. Use phrases such as "when we're at dinner out of the home," "when we're free of distractions," or "when we've been getting enough sleep" as examples.

When are there times when you feel it is safe for you to share your emotions with me?

"This provides you with a great lot of information into the degree of emotional safety and intimacy that exists in the relationship, both of which are essential components of a robust partnership,"

What specific moments from your upbringing bring the greatest happiness to you when you think back on them? Which ones are the most agonizing?

When we make an attempt to avoid experiencing pain, it may often cause a rift in the connection. For instance, if one person came from a household in which birthdays and holidays were a significant source of pleasure, while the other person links same dates with bad memories, this might give rise to conflict or misunderstanding.

Do we appreciate one another's religious beliefs, spiritual practices, and political viewpoints in an acceptable manner?

It's not necessary for partners in a relationship to always see eye to eye on everything. However, you will need to find a method to accept each other's various ideas and identify the things on which you do need to reach a consensus in order to go forward. "Are you both of the same mind about how you think the world should be seen and how people need to be treated? Do you share my thoughts on many political issues? And how essential is it to you to make sure that your belief systems are in line with one another?"

Whose professional life would be put on hold if this were to become necessary?

It's possible that one of you may get a job offer that requires you to relocate across the nation. Or, if there are no longer any child care options, it may be necessary for one of the parents to stop working, as was the case for many families during the influenza pandemic.

Would you support your partner walking away from a job to pursue their ambitions, even if it meant sacrificing family income? "Would you support your spouse walking away from a job to follow their dreams?" You can avoid being taken by surprise in the future by your spouse's opinions about both of your professions if you have a strong knowledge of their attitudes about both of your jobs now. Your partner may regard their professional advancement as taking precedence over yours.

Do either of us have any significant information to ourselves that we have not yet divulged?

It is up to you and your spouse to determine which secrets should be kept a secret, but if you do so, you run the danger of them discovering the secret at a later time. "I've helped couples deal through the revelation of concealed debt, prior infidelity, previous pregnancies, and childhood sexual trauma, I've also assisted couples in working with the discovery of previous pregnancies." "I think it's better to be your genuine honest self and know that you're totally welcomed, regardless of your background," is what I feel to be the best course of action.

Are you willing to provide therapy for us if and when we feel the need for it?

"The number of women I've seen who say that their spouse doesn't 'believe in therapy' or refuses to 'explain their concerns to a stranger' is too high,. "The number of women I've seen who say that their husband doesn't 'believe in counseling' is too high." While you're still basking in the warmth of the pre-engagement period, now is the time to make a game plan for what to do if things go difficult farther down the road.

----------- You should be able to make an educated choice about beginning a life with your partner after going through chapter one of this book and responding to the questions that follow. And if you don't know the answers to any of these questions, use them as a starting point for a conversation with your partner immediately.

However, if you are not fully convinced of the answers to the questions, read chapter 2 below to know what I am talking about.

Chapter 2

What do I mean by a successful Relationship or marriage?

Above in Chapter one, we discussed on "Key questions to ask when getting married" However, as a Relationship counselor, you should not rely on chapter one only. This is what a Successful marriage should look like here.

To the Men

To put it simply, having a nice wife is the most important factor in a happy successful marriage. Most men do the mistake of picking out any kind of lady, picking out any lady from the street is what I call DEATH IN MARRIAGE. I recommend a woman who understands you, support you, and make you have peace of mind. I WOULD SAY MARRY YOUR BEST FRIEND.

The woman is expected to put in all of her effort and pray for the success of the marriage, despite the fact that the husband is the head of the household. If the marriage does not succeed, it is usually the wife's responsibility since she is expected to do so. It is anticipated of her that she would keep the marriage near to her heart. The whole chapter of Proverbs 31 is dedicated to elaborating on what it means to be a lady of virtue. The woman has to treat the marriage as her own personal effort in order to ensure that it is successful. In the 24th verse of the book of Genesis, the man is given the command to turn his back on his parents and cling to his wife, and the two of them will become one flesh.

To The ladies

When it comes to being married, the man should be aware that he is no longer a Mummy's boy, that is one of the most important factors if you want to enjoy a successful marriage, and he should make sure that his parents are kept in the dark about anything that takes place between him and his wife. When they encounter problems, such problems should be addressed without any kind of involvement from a third party. The conflicts that arise between a husband and wife need to be settled by the couple themselves. The speed with which the husband and wife are able to respond to new circumstances and find solutions is what makes the relationship effective. There is no such thing as a perfect marriage since neither of the two people who enter into it are flawless. Because she is the support of the family, the woman is expected to show submission.

Marriage is the union of two persons that results in the formation of a family unit, which has a large amount of importance and weight in the eyes of society as a whole. My view is that a happy marriage is one in which both partners are committed to the idea of bringing up morally upright children who will go on to be productive members of society. If parents were to make a concerted effort to instill moral values in their offspring, there would undoubtedly be more upstanding members of society. In spite of the fact that they come from different families and adhere to different religions, a happy marriage is also dependent on the degree to which the pair understands themselves.

In addition, a happy marriage is one in which there is excellent communication and companionship, in which we are able to speak to each other about anything without any kind of reserve, and in which we are able to spend time together. It is one in which we regard one another as our closest friends, in which we are honest with one another regardless of how unpleasant the reality may be, and in which we do not keep any secrets from one another. The institution of marriage requires a significant amount of giving and receiving of concessions. A happy marriage is not one that is free from conflict or disputes, but it does need both spouses to be modest and self-aware enough to own their mistakes and timely seek forgiveness from one another. Both parties in a marriage eventually become aware of the other's flaws and deficiencies; nevertheless, even with this realization, they shouldn't focus their attention on these things and instead should work to complement one another. Even in the face of criticism, it is best to choose the constructive approach rather than the destructive one. Partners are expected to enjoy spending time in each other's company and look forward to returning to the comfort of their partner's arms at the end of a challenging day.

However, couple should know this that in a marriage, friendship is more important than love; when the first fluttery sensations have passed, it is friendship that keeps the couple together. A relationship built on a strong foundation of trust and self-respect is one of the most important things to look for in a partner. After the couples have established a level of confidence in one another, it will be challenging for a third person to step in between them.

When both partners are willing to accept and accommodate one another, marriage has a better chance of lasting. If two people in a relationship understand one another, then they will be able to accept one another no matter how significant the misunderstanding that arises between them may be. When a marriage is successful, it paves the way for a successful family to be created out of the union. The institution of marriage is developed first, before the establishment of the family unit. Since marriage is the cornerstone upon which a family is built, it stands to reason that if the couple's relationship is healthy, their offspring will be raised in an atmosphere that is highly nurturing and supportive.

Again, a marriage that is successful is a partnership that acknowledges the importance of understanding, commitment, sacrifice, and responsibility. Unconditional love is the single most significant factor in determining whether or not a marriage will be successful. Because no one is flawless, there is a need for love that is not conditional. As a result, it is essential for partners to have an understanding of the shortcomings that each other has. When a couple is together, they should make an effort to better understand one another.

In addition, a happy marriage is one in which the feelings of love, trust, and understanding are maintained in such a manner that they may last from the first day of the marriage till the end of time. A marriage that has weathered the storms of life but maintains trust, love, and understanding between its partners should be considered successful.

In order for a marriage to be successful, both spouses need to have a comprehensive awareness of themselves, including an appreciation of their faults and weaknesses, as well as the ability to compromise through it all.

The keys to a happy marriage are dedication, companionship, open and honest communication. They should be able to openly interact with one another, and both partners should have a strong grasp on who they are. When a couple has reached an agreement with one another, there will be less contention inside the house.

The key to a happy marriage is a partnership that is characterized by complete self-awareness and unwavering confidence in one another by both spouses. Where there is an ongoing symbiotic interaction between them, which means that they are both benefiting from the presence of the other. Honesty and openness are two more important characteristics of a good and successful marriage; when one spouse is honest and open with the other, the marriage is healthy and successful. It is essential for the spouses in a healthy marriage to have an open and honest relationship with one another. Both the woman and the husband need to treat one another like an open book.

If a marriage has all of the above qualities, I will consider it to be successful: peace of mind, respect, excellent communication, patience, support, and kindness of heart; a marriage that even after a very long period still has love and understanding as its basis. In spite of the fact that changes will occur throughout the course of the marriage over time, the husband and wife should encourage and help one another to grow into the subsequent version of themselves, in which they will be able to recognize each other as a single entity.

Chapter 3

Is There A Perfect Relationship?

------------Are You Searching for the Perfect Relationship?

Women often fantasize about having a spouse who is tall, dark, gorgeous, kind, loving, and fun. They want a perfect man who will take care of all of their financial, social, emotional, and spiritual needs. This perfect man would arrive home on time, never drink, never cheat, never flirt, clean up after himself, remember everything (birthdays, anniversaries, etc.), cook for them, and occasionally buy them flowers. In addition, he would be there for them no matter what. A man's perfect spouse should have numerous qualities, including beauty, chastity, loyalty, financial stability, compassion, gentleness, sweetness, delicacy, obedience, adaptability, a focus on the family, and many more. Each of us has a somewhat different concept of the perfect companion. Both are looking for someone they can call "Mr. Perfect" and "Ms. Perfect."

The fact that we want perfection in all of our interactions, despite the fact that we are flawed creatures ourselves, is the greatest irony that comes with being human. There is no such thing as a relationship that is ideal in every way. A perfect relationship is one in which "You live and let live," where there is a profound level of understanding between the two parties, and where each person respects the other's uniqueness.

------------- Guidelines for Having a Perfect Relationship

Acceptance of each other just as they are, including both their positive and negative qualities. Take some time to get your head around the idea that nobody, including you, is flawless. If you still carry about the specter of perfection in your mind, you won't be able to accept the flaws that are present in your relationship.

Love and trust each other. Whether it be a connection between a parent and a kid, a friendship between two individuals, or a partnership between a man and a woman, the development of love and trust is essential to the success of every relationship. Putting in the effort to build trust will eventually result in a scenario in which a youngster will feel comfortable sharing personal information with a parent and a partner will feel at ease discussing whether they had dinner with a guy or a woman without experiencing any anxiety. Love must run so deep in a relationship that even the mere idea of the other person can make you smile, both with your mouth and your heart.

Every relationship needs mutual respect and consideration in order to thrive. There is nothing quite like love that is not conditional. You are going to need to tend to it.

Understanding goes a long way too. When two people who come from different worlds and with distinct histories choose to join together, friction and conflict are inevitable outcomes. Appreciate differences. Adhere to the principle that it is okay to disagree with each other.

Responsibility distribution across all parties. Outside and within the family, men and women should each take on an equal part of the obligations.

Relationships that are ideal always include an ongoing process of compromising and adjusting to one another's needs.

Remember that everyone is their own unique person, and give them room to be themselves. Never, ever make a comparison between your lover and anybody else. When two people are in a healthy relationship with one another, they have a mutual admiration for one another as unique individuals, which enables them to treat one another with respect. When you have respect for someone, it is much simpler to be sensitive of their feelings, patient with them, and to have a high esteem for them. relationship!

The qualities of patience, tolerance, and forgiveness are the pillars around which a healthy and successful relationship is built. Collaborate with your significant other to address any problems that may be affecting the quality of your relationship. Ignore the expectations that society has established for the perfect romantic partnership.

A feeling of belonging to a group and cooperating with others to achieve a shared objective—a life that is joyful and peaceful. In times of difficulty, stick together. People tend to become closer to one another through difficult times, which in turn helps the connection become stronger than it was before.

Maintain your composure despite the ever-changing nature of your connections. It is not a fixed state. You have to put in effort in a relationship on a consistent basis if you want it to become what you see it being and if you want it to endure. It all begins with the physical and continues on to the spiritual.

Having strong debate skills, and they rapidly put an end to conflict. There is no name calling, hitting walls, or throwing items in a relationship that is functioning well. There will be no attacking or pointing the finger here. Instead, they maintain composure, talk things out, refrain from saying or doing things that might be unpleasant, and communicate effectively, which means that they express their thoughts and ideas and listen to each other without passing judgment. They don't want other people to know that they're going through difficulties; it's simply that their disagreements are private and nobody else should be concerned about them.

Being concerned about one another's well-being. People that are self-centered in romantic partnerships run into a lot of difficulties. If both parties in a relationship are focused on their own needs and concerns, then the dynamic is likely to be fraught with tension and hostility. In what seems to be the ideal romantic partnership, both partners are considerate of the emotions and requirements of the other.

Honesty. They may not share all of their ideas with one another, but at the very least, they are honest with one another about what they need from the relationship and how they choose to conduct their life, such as where they went, how they spent the day, and so on.

Maintain Common Interests' There are several partnerships in which the two people involved are so unlike to one another or have drifted so far apart throughout the course of their relationship that they literally do not want to do anything together. There may be two individuals in a great relationship who have a few different hobbies, but there are many activities that they like doing together, and they make it a point to engage in those activities as often as possible so that they may enhance their connection.

Develop your love for one another. People in a great relationship take the time to do things that foster their love for one another, such as complimenting one another, sharing valuable life lessons, laughing with one another, snuggling, holding hands, being nice to one another, and romancing one another.

Being drawn to one another. Two individuals who are attracted to each other and manage to keep that attraction alive via a variety of techniques have the foundation for the ideal relationship. They ensure that the fire is maintained.

Be each other's pillars of support. Your intimate partner is the one person except yourself who should be there for you emotionally and physically as you go through life. They should support you and inspire you to develop into the kind of person you see for yourself. There will be concessions made in order to assist their spouse in accomplishing anything.

Putting one another ahead of themselves. There are things in life that are more essential than others, and it's vital that we keep those things in order. Before their career, their friends, and their interests, the partner in a good relationship comes first in their thoughts and actions. They are willing to provide their spouse with whatever it is that they need, whether it is time, affection, or support. If their spouse is going through a difficult period, they will not spend time having a good time with their friends by going out and hanging out with them. They put their partner's needs above their own and carry out the responsibilities that are necessary for the partner.

Have Faith in One Another Jealousy and uncertainty have no place in a healthy, happy relationship. As a result, they do not draw hasty assumptions about the circumstances. They don't question their companion in great detail about where they were and why they were running behind schedule. In addition, they are able to take their spouse away for a week without being concerned about anything that could occur. The trust is never forced nor difficult; rather, it is just there, and mistrust is not even given a second's consideration.

Don't Keep Anything to Yourself. They don't keep any secrets from one another, which is one reason why they trust one other so much. They are honest with one another about who they are and what they've done during the day, and as a result, their tales never include any contradictions that may lead to suspicion or distrust in the other person. This is one of the many benefits of having a significant other in your life.

Make Each Other Better. Two persons who make the effort to improve one another's mood are essential to the success of any romantic partnership. They do all they can to make the ill person as comfortable as possible, even if it means taking over their housework or other responsibilities for the day. When things go tough, they are there for one another in any manner they might be of assistance. And when their spouse needs someone to speak to or a shoulder to weep on, they are there for them, they are there for their partner.

Having a good rapport with one another. One of the feelings that contributes to maintaining happiness and stability in a relationship is a sense of comfort with the other person. In an ideal relationship, both partners look forward to seeing one other at the end of the day and feel comfortable enough with one another that they can just be themselves anytime they are in the company of their significant other. They do not need to put on an act in order to fool anybody. They are not required to have an excellent demeanor or to be flawless in every way. They are able to be who they are because they have faith that their spouse will accept it and won't make them feel awful about themselves.

The liberty to be able to spend time by oneself There is no such thing as a perfect relationship if the two people in it are forced to spend all of their time together. The simple fact that people are unique individuals means that they require space to pursue their own interests in order to maintain their emotional, mental, and spiritual health. If they are not given this space, they are likely to experience feelings of emptiness and dissatisfaction on some level.

A sense of parity or equality In a relationship, there should never be a situation in which one person is the subordinate or slave of the other. This may lead to sentiments of wrath, resentment, and sadness, all of which are detrimental to the health of a relationship. Two persons who respect and value one another equally are necessary for a healthy and happy relationship.

They interact and play with one another. Your connection may be strengthened by engaging in lighthearted interaction with one another. Additionally, it might assist you in making each other laugh out loud. Having a good sense of humor is consistently ranked as one of the most appealing traits in both men and women; hence, it is a very desirable quality to have in a relationship.

They Are Willing to Admit When They Are Wrong Neither one of them is willing to take the time to acknowledge and forgive their errors.

There is no one way that all relationships can be improved in the same way. Because each individual is so genetically unique, there is no one rule that can be applied to everyone. To have healthy and happy relationships, one must put forth the effort to cultivate and maintain them. This calls for a great deal of self-reflection and investigation. There need to be a sincere resolve on your part to make your life successful and joyful. A perfect relationship does not mean that the couple has never disagreed about anything, that they have never had relationship problems, or that they have never raised their voices in anger toward one another; rather, it means that in a perfect relationship, all differences, disputes, and conflicts are so well handled with the tools of tolerance, patience, forgiveness, and mutual respect. They become skilled in the "Agree to Disagree" art form.

Chapter 4

10 Marriage Tips every wife needs to know

Now listen! This is one of the important chapters in this book, and you don't want to take it for granted. To have a happy relationship in your home, every woman needs to know this. This is basically for the women and if you are a man, there is no limit for you too. Likewise, it would be advisable if you could perhaps teach your wife.

As a woman who is getting married, you will find that marriage is very different from how you expected it to be when you were a teenager, when you fantasized about meeting your "Prince Charming" and living happily ever after. Real marriage, despite the fact that it comes with its fair share of romantic and lovey-dovey moments, is labor-intensive.

Note: If you are already married, put these suggestions into order, and within a short period of time, you will undoubtedly begin to witness wonderful and pleasant changes in your family life.

-----------The Top 10 Pieces of Advice Every Wife Should Hear About Their Marriage

1. RESPECT

The most important thing for a guy is to be respected by others, and the woman he marries should be the one from whom he craves respect the most. Respect and trust are two things that must be earned, which is something that we are all aware of, but there must be a starting point from which we all operate. There must be a minimum foundation of respect that is there at all times, regardless of the circumstances, simply because you have committed to spending the rest of your lives with each other and have spoken your vows to each other with sincerity.

And the reality is that over the life of your marriage, both you and your husband will make mistakes on a regular basis. Nobody is without flaws. There is no other context in which the practice of forgiveness is more essential or more difficult than in the context of the married relationship.

2. Learn the love language that he speaks.

One of the most thoughtful things you can do for your marriage is to get an understanding of both your own and your partner's primary modes of expressing and receiving love. This is one of the nicest gifts you can offer them. Words of Affirmation, Quality Time Spent Together, Gifts Considered, Acts of Service Rendered, and Physical Touch Are Considered to Be the Five Primary Love Languages

3. Make time for your significant other.

It is not true that after you are married, you are no longer allowed to date each other like in the past. It certainly shouldn't. The beginning of a romantic relationship can be found in the smallest gestures, such as preparing his favorite French toast for breakfast on the weekends or surprise him with lunch at his place of work. Make anniversaries, birthdays, and random days in between into memorable one-on-one dates with your significant other.

Naturally, this will be more difficult for you to do if you have children, but there is always the option of hiring a babysitter. If you can manage it, try to avoid talking constantly about things like your children, the chores you have around the home, or the money situation in your household. Instead, discuss your anxieties, plan your next vacation together, share your ambitions, or try out a new pastime together.

4. Effective communication is essential

The majority of issues that arise in romantic partnerships can be traced back to a breakdown in communication. When it comes to a marriage, there is no alternative for open and honest communication. Never make the assumption that your spouse will be able to read between the lines or that he will know what you want him to do, feel, or say. Don't beat about the bush or arbitrarily drop clues; just be direct and say things as they are. Simply let him know that you need him to step up and do his part of the housekeeping if you want him to do so. Saying anything like "I didn't have time to wash the laundry today yet" and then becoming offended when he doesn't volunteer to do it is unnecessary; instead, just say something like "I couldn't finish the laundry today." Could you assist me in carrying it out?

5. Keep your heart safe.

Your husband's ultimate goal is not only to rule the home; rather, he yearns to rule over your emotions and your whole being. You promised to give your whole heart to one guy for the rest of your life when you exchanged vows at your wedding. When it comes down to it, now is the moment to keep your word and honor the promise you made. Although there is nothing inherently wrong with having a best friend forever or a small group of close friends, you should take care to protect your heart and avoid being too emotionally attached to any anyone other than your spouse.

This is true regardless of whether the friends in question are male or female; nonetheless, the stakes are much higher in the event that a male buddy is involved. When emotions are allowed to run wild and unregulated, things can change in the blink of an eye. This is something that no one anticipates happening at the beginning of the situation.

6. Allow your "Yes" to mean what it says and your "No" to mean what it says

In many aspects of life, but especially in marital relationships, telling the truth is always the best strategy. Ladies, we sometimes give evasive answers when we are uncomfortable with the truth or when we don't want to appear pushy or demanding, but the fact of the matter is that your husband wants to know your genuine opinion on things, not just what sounds good. This is because your husband values honesty more than he values appearing pushy or demanding. We've all been in the scenario when we agreed to do something for the purpose of keeping our spouse happy, but deep inside, we disliked being dragged into it. This is something that happens to all of us. Over the course of time, irritation and a loss of confidence can develop from seemingly little occurrences like these.

7. Give him room to breathe

It is important for women to have time to themselves for activities such as retail therapy, periodic pampering sessions at the spa, and time spent catching up with their companions. Even men have to take some time for themselves. On the other hand, it's possible that they don't "get it" in the same way that we do. A good number of wives see the importance of their men taking some time for themselves at the end of the workday, away from the pressures of their jobs and the obligations of family life, to do whatever it is that re-energizes them.

For some, it can be nothing more than reading the latest news online, while for others, it might be playing video games for half an hour. Working mothers, you are just as worn out as your spouse is and have just as much need for some personal space. The most important thing is to acknowledge that you BOTH need to carve out this time for yourselves on a regular basis and to have a plan for how to work it into the schedules of the other members of your family.

8. Show an interest in the things that fascinate him.

Find out more about the things he enjoys doing. You are not required to necessarily accompany him on the (video game) battlefield or on those long bicycle journeys (although you may do so!), but you should take the time to grasp what the game is about or how the guys prepare for their nightly expeditions. Find out what type of movies and music he likes, as well as what activities he used to like doing but has since given up. The process of getting to know one another does not finish with marriage; rather, it is just getting started.

9. Devote some of your time to getting to know his loved ones and close friends.

When you married the guy, you also brought his friends and family into your life, which is a significant change. His old life, including his family and friends, will continue to coexist with his new life with you in the same way that your old life includes your family and friends. Therefore, if you haven't already done this before to getting married, make it a priority to familiarize yourself with the important individuals in your man's life. It's important to him in more ways than you would realize.

10. Refrain from making disparaging remarks about your partner.

Conflicts in marriage are an inevitable part of the journey; yet, the ancient adage "Don't hang your dirty laundry out to dry" has a lot of relevance in the modern world. When it comes to discussing the problems and incidents in our marriages with our girlfriends, we ladies have a propensity to gossip and may get carried away. Avoid having these talks at all costs, despite the fact that it may be tempting to do so in order to obtain the support and encouragement you need. First and foremost, you need to consider the reaction that your partner might have if he or she overheard any of these talks.

Second, put yourself in his shoes and consider how you would react if he was talking about you in the same way. Thirdly, when you put such things out into the open, there is no way of knowing for certain how the other person will interpret what has been revealed or what they will do with the knowledge. This is because there is no way of knowing how the other party will use the information. And last, the more you speak about it, the more likely it is that you will get outraged at the (see) unfairness or unjust treatment that you have gotten, and this is something that is not going to help you settle the matter any more effectively.

---------Having said about the women, regardless men are not left out....Men should know that they have their role to play in the marriage as; therefore, this would be discussed in the next chapter below - ***10 Things a Man should know about marriage***

Chapter 5

10 Marriage Tips every man needs to know

Marriage is not about having that picture-perfect home, an adorable brood, and hearty home-cooked meals every day, although those things can be the icing on the cake. Contrary to the many romantic movies you may have seen with your significant other, marriage is not about having that picture-perfect home. A true marriage requires a lot of effort. There may probably be times when you feel like you simply can't comprehend the lady you married, and you'll be at a total lost as to what to do in such situations.

----------------- The top 10 things every man should know

1. L-O-V-E

The most important thing for a woman is to be loved, whereas the most important thing for a guy is to be respected. It is not necessary to have a big party in order to show that you care about someone, but showing love should be an intrinsic part of your day-to-day existence. In the eyes of a woman, love is almost never just about sexual intimacy. Every little thing you do, from the way you talk to her in private and in public to whether or not you contribute to the management of duties at home to the amount of time you spend together on the weekends, may all say a great deal about you to your wife. It is inevitable that there will be times when your wife will seem to be unlovable; this might be as a result of harsh words being said or a request that looks unreasonable being made; nonetheless, it is important to keep in mind that no one is flawless. Keep in mind that you promised to love and cherish each other "through thick and thin" when you were married.

2. Learn how she like to be loved.

One of the most thoughtful things you can do for your marriage is to get an understanding of both your own and your partner's primary modes of expressing and receiving love. This is one of the nicest gifts you can offer them. Words of Affirmation, Quality Time Spent Together, Gifts Considered, Acts of Service Rendered, and Physical Touch Are Considered to Be the Five Primary Love Languages.

3. Be kind to her and show her respect at all times.

Even the most self-reliant and confident of women want for a companion who would treat them with kindness and consideration at all times. It is not out of a misplaced sense of male superiority that views his wife as weak and powerless, nor is it out of a fear of provoking her fury, but rather out of a sincere desire to honor his wife and set a good example for their marriage.

4. Listen well

The majority of men have an innate ability to solve problems and tend to lean toward finding a solution to every issue that arises, even the problems that your wife is having. On the other hand, the majority of women aren't as focused on finding a solution to their issues as they are on finding someone to go through life with them and share the experience. Your wife is looking more for your empathy than she is for your advice. She does not want you to dismiss her concerns as "trivial," but rather for you to put down the newspaper and pay attention to what she has to say. First and foremost, gentlemen, you should perfect the art of attentively listening to your wives or husbands.

5. Make time for your significant other.

It is not true that after you are married, you are no longer allowed to go for dates. Sparks of romance that were so much a part of your courting may sometimes be snuffed out by the regular routine of everyday life, and it will require work from both sides to keep the flame alive after the sparks have been extinguished. It's the small things that count when it comes to creating a romantic atmosphere at home, like serving her breakfast in bed or surprise her with a bouquet of her favorite flowers. Make anniversaries, birthdays, and random days in between into memorable one-on-one dates with your significant other. Set aside some time to discuss your anxieties, plan your next vacation, speak about your hopes, and maybe try out a new pastime together. Make the most of the time you have together.

6. Effective communication is essential

The majority of issues that arise in romantic partnerships can be traced back to a breakdown in communication. When it comes to a marriage, there is no alternative for open and honest communication. Many wives make the mistake of expecting that their husbands are able to read between the lines or will know what to do, feel, or say in response to what they have communicated with them. This is a dangerous assumption to make. On the other hand, many men choose the approach of "telling it like it is." There will be instances when your thoughts and actions get confused. Husbands, don't give up! Even while it may be irritating at times to attempt to "read" your wife, it is important to keep trying since communication is really an art form that can only be perfected after a great deal of time and experience. Simply making the effort matters more to her than you probably realize at this point.

7. Take turns being responsible for the household

It takes two hands to form a fist, and it will require the combined efforts of both partners in the marriage to turn the house into a home. To be clear, not every guy is cut out to be a house husband, nor should he be expected to be, but the fact that males are male does not free them from the responsibility of doing housekeeping. This is particularly relevant in modern times since the majority of homes have two working members. Because your wife is just as worn out as you are at the conclusion of a hard day at work, it is unreasonable to expect her to shoulder the majority of the responsibilities associated with maintaining the home. And men, if your wife is a Stay-at-Home-Mum, know that she has not been lying on the couch shaking her legs all day

— the work of mothering is one of the roughest occupations there is. The job of being a mother is one of the hardest professions there is.

8. Devote some of your time to getting to know her loved ones and close friends.

It's okay if you don't get along with every single member of your wife's family or circle of friends; you don't have to. However, now that you're married, it would mean the world to your wife if you would at least make an effort to get acquainted with the people who are so significant to her. Therefore, if you haven't already done this before to getting married, make it a priority to familiarize yourself with these important individuals in your wife's life.

9. Avoid comparing yourself to others.

When it comes to marriage, comparison is one of the biggest enemies of happiness. Fight the temptation to compare your wife to the partners of your friends or to figures in movies or television shows. There is no such thing as a flawless guy, and the same is true of women. This is extremely risky when it comes to a man's sexual fantasies, and it's one of the primary reasons why so many married men resort to porn to satiate their appetites for sexual escapism. And yet, by doing so, they are, in effect, spoiling the real sexual experience that they have for themselves, which will, in the end, have a negative impact on the relationship.

10. She does not have you as her father.

One of the most emotionally charged moments of a wedding often occurs when the father of the bride gives her hand in marriage to the man she has loved throughout his life. It is possible for a man to have the impression that he has been entrusted with a rare treasure that he is responsible for guarding and preserving, and in some ways, he really has. On the other hand, there are moments when a concern may morph into excessive protection, and leadership can morph into tyranny. Always keep in mind that your wife already has a father, and that you are not that man for her. Instead of treating your wife like a kid who is in need of your parental control, husbands should love, respect, defend, and support their wives as equals.

Even after following these tips as a couple, many complaint I have gotten are Mostly "ROMANCE" ------------------ This is a huge factor that can lead to death in marriage -------

In the Following chapter, we will discuss on **Reasons there is no romance in your relationship and how you can solve them.**

Chapter 6

Romance in Relationship

A relationship where there is no romance is mostly likely to be dead. Romance should always be a priority in a relationship, regardless of how long the couple has been together, whether it six months, six years, or even longer.

It is the essential energy source that keeps a connection going in the right direction. It maintains the relationship's vitality, excitement, and significance. When your lover does something romantic for you, it makes you feel wanted, cherished, and cared for. They serve as a gentle but powerful reminder that your spouse has not only chosen you but also values having you in their lives.

If you are not getting romance in your relationship, here are the reasons;

What to do when romance has died in a marriage and there is no more romance in a relationship is discussed in the following paragraphs.

How things work out

How did your relationship go from being romantic to being completely void of passion after you were married? During the first few months or years of a new partnership, the development of romantic feelings is completely normal and healthy. When two people are trying to win one another's affection, they seek for methods to make one other feel unique and special, and romanticism is one approach that is often used. During the "puppy love" period of any relationship, it is standard practice to shower one another with thoughtful presents, go on dates, and cook up something special for supper.

Unless your spouse is naturally passionate, this romanticism may start to wane throughout the course of your relationship as time goes on. This is a natural consequence of being at ease in the relationship and no longer feeling the need to impress the other person. On the other hand, there is no romance and no passion in the relationship for either of you. In the absence of love, a relationship loses all of the color and beauty that it once had. This was originally there in your marriage.

Has he ever shown a romantic side?

In contrast to what was said above, it's possible that your spouse was never romantic in the first place. In point of fact, many individuals complain that their primary issue is "my boyfriend is not romantic" or "my spouse has no love for me," and this is a regular problem that they encounter.

If this is the case, and if your desire for greater romance in your relationship has not been met with a positive response, you may need to come to terms with the fact that he is not romantic, and that he is just not the sort of person you anticipate him to be. The fact that he expresses his passion for you in other ways is not evidence that he does not love or want you; rather, it is just a reflection of the fact that a relationship does not include romance

---------------------Implications of a lack of romance in a relationship

It may seem absurd to most people for a woman to be unhappy about the absence of romance in her relationship, but the emotional side effects of not having romance in a relationship may cause problems. When there is a lack of romanticism in a relationship, it may lead to marital discord between the couple.

If your spouse is not the romantic or loving kind, then the two of you may feel more like roommates than lovers due to the lack of intimacy and romanticism in your relationship. The following are some of the consequences that arise when you cease trying to win over your partner's affections.

An absence of romance, particularly in a sexual sense, has the potential to make a woman experience feelings of insecurity. She can't help but ponder whether or not her partner considers her to be emotionally or physically arousing.

When a woman is not physically appealing, she can begin to question whether or not her partner still finds her attractive. This might be particularly unpleasant if she has undergone substantial physical transformations since the beginning of the relationship.

This insecurity may lead to melancholy or acting out in destructive ways, including seeking affirmation and praise from another guy, which are both unhealthy responses to the situation.

Is he trying to con me? Whether her guy has stopped showering her with the same level of romanticism that he used to, she may start to worry if he is paying attention to another woman instead of her.

-----------**What to do in a relationship when there is no longer any romance**

Even if there is no romance in a relationship, this does not always indicate that the relationship is unhealthy. In all other elements of your life, your partner may be a great provider, parent, and attentive companion; nevertheless, he is not giving you romance.

What to do when there is no romance in your love life is outlined in the following.

Spend some time with one another.

Increasing the amount of time that you spend together paves the way for several romantic possibilities. Keep in mind that there is more to your relationship than merely doing things together every day. Have fun together. Participate in a game in which you and your partner each ask one another one hundred questions about the other's life. Pretend as if you are just starting out as a couple. This will not only make your spouse feel unique, but it will also provide you the chance to share information about yourself and strengthen your connection. Taking up a new hobby or pastime together is another fantastic approach to strengthen relationships. The more you have in common with one another, the simpler it will be to develop a love connection between the two of you.

Promote closeness and companionship

One of the more apparent ways to infuse more romance into a relationship is to fabricate circumstances that encourage increased levels of closeness. The following are some suggestions for incorporating more romance into your life on a daily basis.

Connect with one another during sexual activity: Sexual activity provides the ideal setting for romantic interaction. This does not imply that you have to play out the sexual encounter like a scene from a movie; rather, you should focus on maintaining a connection with your partner while engaging in sexual activity. This includes making kissing sounds, holding hands, and making direct eye contact.

Text: Start sending and receiving text messages to one another throughout the day. It may be less challenging to express one's romantic feelings via writing than it is to do so verbally at times.

Simply by holding hands with one another, you may create a stronger connection. When it comes to a relationship, the importance of physically touching one another outside of the bedroom cannot be overstated. Hug one another, get up and dance, get cozy on the sofa, and play footsies. Try to include some kind of physical contact into whatever it is that the two of you are doing.

Combine to form a harmonious whole: One strategy that may be used to create a sense of exclusivity for both you and your spouse is to go out of your way to complement one another. It might be as easy as saying "You look beautiful today" or as complex as expressing gratitude for XYZ and expressing how much it meant to you.

Give presents. This is an option that is by no means required for the creation of romance; nonetheless, it is a kind gesture that will make your spouse want to return the favor. Your significant other will place a high value on an unexpected present, even if it is something simple but meaningful.

Small surprises in the form of presents or kind acts should be exchanged.

It is not necessary for these to be showy or costly.

These seemingly insignificant gestures can pack a significant romantic punch because they convey the message "I'm thinking of you." For example, a simple love note written on a post-it note and placed next to his briefcase or a surprise pizza delivery to her office at lunchtime when you know she is pressed for time and unable to leave the building are both examples.

Have some fun with your companion.

That's correct; you should flirt with your partner in marriage. Have you completely forgotten about that vanished kind of art?

If you have discovered a definitive answer to the topic of whether or not romance is necessary in marriage, then you probably already know that there are very few things more romantic than engaging in some sexual flirtation with one another.

While you two are brushing your teeth together in the evening, use the opportunity to flirt with one another. (Perhaps a little squeeze on the buttocks, or a sneaky hand stroking his sensitive areas?)

When you are getting comfortable to watch your favorite program with your significant other, put your hand on their leg and give them a little squeeze as a flirtatious move. Text each other and flirt with one other throughout the day... "I can't wait to roll over and snuggle up next to you in bed tonight!"

You will have a better understanding of the significance of romance in a relationship by reading all of these things, and you will also be able to recall what it was like to be in the early stages of love, when romance was at its peak and you couldn't keep your hands off of each other.

Bring it back!

Express to your partner the reasons you adore them.

In addition to using the straightforward phrase "I love you," there are numerous more methods in which you may express your love to your lover. You may say something like, "I adore how you take such wonderful care of all of us," "I love how you smell," or "I appreciate that you remember to take the recycling out every week." These are all great ways to show appreciation.

The purpose of this is to convey to your spouse that you are aware of them, that you value them, and that you do not take them for granted in any way.

Seek assistance

A lack of romanticism in a relationship may not seem to be a significant concern to other observers, but it can be a source of insecurity for the partner who is not made to feel like they are essential in the relationship. It's possible that getting therapy might be beneficial for your relationship as a whole.

Get in touch with a doctor: If you suspect that your low libido is the cause of your lack of romantic fulfillment, it is in your best interest to get in touch with your primary care physician. They will be able to tell you the root cause of the problem, whether it is due to a shift in hormone levels or an emotional distance between the two of you. Either outcome will assist the two of you in making a decision on your next steps as a pair.

Marriage therapy may assist couples in being more emotionally connected to one another and in determining the origin of the challenges they are encountering in their connection to one another.

Don't be scared to go forward and take the initiative.

It's common for women to defer to their partners when it comes to romantic endeavors, but you should never be hesitant to take the initiative. Find methods to show your spouse that you care in ways that he will find meaningful. Pay attention to the things that he values. Keep in mind that what he finds romantic may not be something that you find romantic at all. Both surprising him with a present or taking him to a place that was special to him when he was a youngster are thoughtful ways to express that you care. When he realizes that you are the one who is leading the romantic charge, he will likely start looking for methods to return the favor.

It is possible to have a happy and fulfilling relationship that lasts for a long time if both couples remember how important it is to keep the romantic aspect of the relationship alive, to make the other person feel loved, and to bring happiness into their lives.

When a relationship loses its romantic spark, the inevitable result is a severing of all ties and the end of the partnership altogether.

It is impossible to place enough emphasis on the significance of romance inside a partnership. Romance is the spark that maintains a couple's connection to one another and the ardor they have for one another.

When you see and feel that your relationship is heading down the path of irritation and relationship satisfaction, put a stop to it and ask yourself why romance is so vital in a relationship.

Happiness and fulfillment are the rewards that come to couples that put in the work to maintain the spark of romance in their relationship.

Don't thus allow the monotony of everyday life to diminish the significance of keeping the romance alive in your relationship.

Chapter 7

Romantic things to do for your partner

It's that time of year when everyone seems to be in the mood for love... On Valentine's Day, why not go the extra mile and do something kind for the person you're in a relationship with?

Post-It Notes

You may try to leave your loved one charming tiny notes tucked away in discrete locations all throughout the home, such as in their shoe cabinet, dresser, or even the refrigerator, so that they are reminded of your affection for them anytime they go to utilize those areas. You could even write something that is pertinent to the hiding area, such as "Thank you for always preparing me such delicious meals," and put it in the refrigerator. Just your honest reflections, straight from the core of your being, without any flowery language or drawn-out narratives.

Breakfast in Bed

It is true that the weekends are a great opportunity for all of us to make up for lost sleep, and it may be difficult to drag oneself out of bed and into the kitchen in the small hours of the morning to make breakfast. On the other hand, love is always a decision. If your significant other knew that you got up earlier to make them a delicious breakfast, I'm sure the expression on their face would be more than enough of a reward for all of the hard work you put in, and I'm sure it would be. It is not necessary to prepare a full English breakfast if you do not like to do so; a meal consisting of toast, cereal, and milk can satisfy your appetite just as well.

Organize a Holiday Surprise for Someone.

You should try to arrange for an unexpected vacancy all by yourself, including the choice of place, the booking of flight tickets and accommodations, the taking of leave for your spouse if they are working on their behalf, the packing of baggage, and so on. If it is at all feasible, you should spring the surprise on a weekday while they are getting ready for work. When you do this, you should bring out their baggage, offer them their passport, and exclaim, "Baby, we're going on vacation!" Your surprise is definitely going to be one that your loved one thinks back on.

Massage

After a long and stressful day of work, there is no better way to say "I Love You" than with a full body massage. The best part is that you won't need much effort to do this! There is neither a need for preparation nor expenditures.

Affirmations of Confidence

It's easy to take the person you've been with for a long time for granted once you've been with them for a while, especially if you've been living with. You should make an effort to show your spouse how much you appreciate them, and you should remember to specifically specify the activities in which you valued their assistance. This will allow them to feel acknowledged for the effort and hard work they have been putting in all this time.

Hi darling, All of the duties around the home have been completed.

Take a break from work for a few hours and pitch in to assist your significant other with the housework. They are going to be overjoyed when they return to a spotless house that has all of the goods they need loaded up in the refrigerator.

Take one step at a time as you go down Memory Lane.

Do you both recall where you initially made eye contact with one another? Which came first: the first movie you watched as a couple or the first meal you had together? Recall the seemingly little moments of your romance that turned out to be crucial in the end while you lie in bed sipping a glass of wine and reminiscing with your significant other.

Simply because I care, I'm sending an arrangement of flowers...

Simply because you care, you should send your sweetheart a flower arrangement or any other present that you believe they would like receiving. There are no specific events to commemorate; all that matters is that you adore them.

Hugs from behind

Hugs from behind, that is all there is to say.

Late-night dates

Remember those late-night dates you used to go on when you were in the dating scene? Relive those carefree days by throwing up a spontaneous date night and doing anything the two of you want to do! You could go to the beach and take in the fresh air, or you could visit that strange little café that's been lurking around the neighborhood that you've always been curious about.

Chapter 8

Good sexual communication

Many married couples acknowledge that they struggle to communicate about sexual matters, whether it is before, during, or after sexual activity. This is often the result of a pessimistic outlook on sexual activity, a concern that they may get a hostile response from their partner or, more generally, a fundamental lack of self-assurance in approaching the topic.

The following are four methods that can help you improve your sexual communication, and with some practice and some time, ideally, it will become easier for you to have honest discussions concerning the subject of sex:

Determine the message that you want to convey.

Do give some attention to the specific message that you want to get over to the recipient. When you have sex, do you experience any pain? Could it be that the same old thing is getting to you? Or do you just realize that sexual activity may be more enjoyable if...

One thing I constantly tell people is that if you don't ask for something, you won't receive it. If you don't know what it is that you want, you can't ask for it. If you don't know who you are, it's impossible to know what you desire. You have to take responsibility for your body as well as your experiences and your sexuality. Don't simply brush aside your sexual pleasure in the hopes that things would get better with time since there's a chance that they won't.

Declare your purpose here.

What should you do when you have decided what it is that you want to say and have succeeded in getting your partner's undivided attention? You may lessen the impact of any consequences by announcing your purpose early. In a nutshell, you need to answer the question: why are you sharing this? Why should we care about this? Why should he even bother paying attention?

If all you want to know is why your spouse performs a certain action, you may say something like, "Sweetheart, I have been wanting to ask you..." (You are inquisitive.)

Or, if you believe that sexuality has become a problem, you may state, "Darling, I am scared discussing this with you. I hope you don't take this the wrong way." On the other hand, I believe it is essential for me to be truthful since I am well aware that I would like it if you were truthful with me... (I assume that being honest is your objective.)

Elaborate

Have you ever heard the expression, "It is not what you say; it is how you say it?" It is my recommendation that you worry less about the precise phrase and instead concentrate more on the goal, and as a result, the way your words sound (or your tone of voice). The more transparent your aim is, the higher the probability that the significance of what you are trying to convey will be understood.

Another piece of advice is that no one can ever disprove what you believe, how you feel about something, or what you perceive in your body since these are all products of your own personal experiences. Use "I" phrases to take ownership of your experience rather than pointing fingers or using accusatory language. Begin your sentence with "I feel..."

Clarify

In your introduction, in addition to establishing the appropriate goal (including your tone), you could also choose to include open-ended or closed-ended questions.

Some examples include the question, "What do you think?" (Open-ended), or "Were you experiencing any discomfort?" You should probably steer clear of asking inquiries such as "Are you in agreement?"

Even if your first try does not go as intended, you are already a winner for making the effort to push through your fear of speaking out or talking about sex. Even if your first attempt does not go as planned, you are still a winner. Regroup. Think about what you intended to say as well as what your partner believed you meant. How might I better understand what you mean? Were you trying to be overly dominant? Check to see whether you were being a pest. There are instances when less might really be more.

After the seed was planted, this idea or notion needs some time to develop into something more fully formed. Additionally, in some circumstances, it may take some time to stop a habit of behavior. Your viewpoint ought to become more clear to others if you repeat it in a subtle way. When everything else fails, you may want to think about seeking the assistance of an objective third party, such as a marital counselor or a sexologist, to help you and your partner improve your ability to communicate with one another or to address your sexual difficulties head-on. However, the first step is to make an attempt to contact them. I really hope that this has inspired some thoughts in you.

Chapter 9

Keep the romance alive

When the expenses start building up, the children require additional care, that is if there are kids in the picture already, and work is demanding more time, couples often have a tendency to forget about the romance in their relationship.

It is natural for spouses to put themselves last in order to prioritize the requirements of the household. This could sometimes lead to more serious relationship problems as the neglect of romance could gradually build that dividing wall between them until that time when they would get drowned in other priorities and would forget their roles as the other half of their spouse. This could sometimes lead to more serious relationship problems as the neglect of romance could gradually build that dividing wall between them.

There are various things that a couple can do to keep the romance alive even though they are working hard to take care of other duties, including the following:

Remember the occasion of your anniversary. One way to appreciate the time you have spent together over the years is to reflect on the beginning of your journey as a couple. You will then make it a goal to maintain longer engagements, which will enable you to reflect on the highs and lows that you have experienced in the past.

Every once in a while, you should both try your hand at slow dancing. This not only helps couples get more intimate with one another but also has a resetting effect on both mood and perspective towards the relationship.

Find some time to get away from everything, including your children, and enjoy some time to yourself. Your relationships with one another as couples would be strengthened and your commitment to one another would be renewed via the experience of spending time together on a vacation cruise. This is a sufficient opportunity for you to catch up on the latest goings-on at work and among your friends and family members.

Send your spouse an unexpected lunch treat in the mail. This might be seen as a very significant message, particularly if you are aware that your spouse is currently dealing with a backlog of office work.

Show consideration for the requirements of one another. The absence of proper care is what drives the other person away. Consequently, regardless of the difficulty of the situation, you should make an effort to find the opportunity to inquire about his or her workday. Asking your spouse straightforward inquiries like this one demonstrates that you are interested in the activities they are participating in.

Please apologize. Even if you don't believe you did anything wrong, apologizing in a genuine manner will demonstrate that you are capable of humbling yourself for the sake of the relationship.

▪ Write a love letter. Even though love letters are an outdated form of communication, there is no better method to convey your feelings than via the written word. Letters provide a discrete channel for expressing sentiments that have been suppressed and unspoken for a long time.

If you are going to be together, it doesn't matter what you are doing as long as fantastic love songs are playing in the background. The result is the creation of a swoon-worthy ambiance everywhere.

Make your lover feel special by giving them kisses. Keep the flames of passion alive by kissing and touching your partner often. The monotony of the day may be broken up with the help of a simple peck on the cheek.

You should never go to bed with an unresolved disagreement. Make a concerted effort to sleep quietly next to one another whenever you can. Couples that don't give each other cause for anxiety will find that each new day brings them joy.

Enjoy yourselves sexually. In healthy and happy relationships, sexual intimacy plays an essential role.

All of these things, in addition to your pledge of constancy, will undoubtedly strengthen the romantic connection that you and your partner have and help you to maintain that connection over time.

By implementing all these tips, I believe it is should have been able to solve 90% in every relationship problem. However, they say; a **relationship without fight is a fake one; sometimes it's good for a relationship to have Fights in them for a stronger connection.**

But, Keeping the words, fight and nurturing the argument is a big NO in a relationship, it doesn't have any good advantage in a relationship.

We will discuss **Tips to deal with couple fights** in the next chapter.

Chapter 10

Tips to deal with couple Fights wisely

The presence of a companion does not guarantee a fun time all the time. If not managed properly, the unique differences that exist between two individuals have the potential to lead to unintended misunderstandings and disputes that are destructive to both parties. Despite the fact that a couple may have loved each other for a long time, disagreements over views and preferences may still lead to conflict and tense situations. When a conflict between a couple is about to start, it is smart for both parties to take some precautions against it.

There are a lot of different factors that might lead to arguments between partners in a relationship. Fights between spouses can be triggered by a wide variety of factors, including but not limited to differences in priorities, perspectives, and financial situations. The following is a list of unfavorable circumstances, along with some advice on how to deal with them:

Battles Over Money

It's common for couples to argue about financial matters because they struggle to trust each other in other areas of their relationship. It's possible that one of them isn't being responsible enough, so the other tries to take leadership. It's possible that they have different perspectives on how money should be valued. Couples have a responsibility to discuss their worries and formulate a game plan for the family's financial situation. Only married couples should consider combining their financial resources into a single account called a joint account. It's important for couples to stay together through the tough times as well as the good moments.

The Distribution of Duties around the House

In the past, it was often expected of females to run the whole family, but in today's more egalitarian society, it is vital for the husband and wife to divide up the domestic responsibilities fairly between themselves. Create a plan, and then stick to it. Focus your energy on finding ways to make your partner's life easier so that you don't have to worry about how you can take advantage of the other person.

Sexual Conflicts

The pair may have different tastes regarding the frequency and length of sexual encounters due to the fact that they partake in different activities on a daily basis. Before allowing oneself to feel deprived or unwelcome, partners in a relationship should first show a deep level of empathy for their partner's situation. If one spouse does not make enough time for sexual activities with the other, that partner should make up for it by devoting more time to the relationship overall.

Kids

Couples often argue over how best to raise and care for their children. When it comes to disciplining children, a problem arises when one parent is more lax than the other. It is important for partners to learn how to put their own preferences aside for the sake of the children in their care. They need to institute regulations that are advantageous to the children rather than those that benefit their own powers.

Diverse Anticipations and Hopes

It's possible that your spouse had a really skewed impression of who you are, in contrast to who you truly are. It is in everyone's best interest to put their cards on the table and be completely honest with their partners about what they can and cannot expect from them before getting into a heated disagreement. Using coercion to bring about change seldom results in positive outcomes. Never make the mistake of trying to mold another person into your image.

Fights between partners may, like any other kind of disagreement, be addressed most effectively when both parties speak with one another. Spending quality time with one another and being able to be honest with one another can help heal wounds and strive for a deeper comprehension of one another's requirements.

The Methods of Fighting

Conflict is something that a lot of people work hard to avoid, but according to my findings, every conflict is really a chance to make a connection stronger. The most important thing is to acquire the skill of learning how to argue in a manner that is not only productive but also makes you feel better about your spouse.

John Gottman, a researcher specializing in marriage, has made his whole career out of analyzing the dynamics of couple hood. He was surprised to discover that couples are prepared to voice their problems even in a controlled environment such as a laboratory, even while scientists are observing and the cameras are rolling. As a result of this study, he devised a method of categorizing words and gestures that has been proved to be highly predictive of a couple's likelihood of success in their relationship as well as their likelihood of divorcing or otherwise breaking up.

One of the most significant studies that Dr. Gottman and his colleagues conducted included observing recently married couples while they were in the middle of an argument. He realized that neither the nature of the argument nor its length had any bearing on the outcome of the conflict. What was the single most accurate indicator of the state of the couple's marriage? The findings of the study showed that a prediction of a couple's likelihood of divorce over the following six years could be made after evaluating only the first three minutes of an argument between them.

This is wonderful news for couples since it provides a space for the two of you to concentrate your attention. During an argument, the initial few minutes, when you and your spouse are still on good terms but the issue is only heating up, are the most significant moments between the two of you. If you put your attention on how you act at that period, you will probably be able to improve the way that your relationship functions as a result.

The following are some of the most effective ways to argue with the person you love:

Find the complaint, not the criticism, and focus on it. Do not begin an argument with your spouse by criticizing them by saying, "You never help me," even if you are irritated about the chores. Pay attention to the issue and the solutions that will help it. When I get home after working late on Thursdays, it is very difficult to see the kids not showered and the dishes not done. Do you believe there's any way you might discover to be of additional assistance on those nights?"

Avoid "you" expressions. Criticism and blame nearly usually follow phrases like "you always" and "you never," which are direct addresses to the speaker.

Consider the use of pronouns. Instead of placing blame on another person, trying beginning your sentences with "I" or "We." This can help you recognize issues and possible solutions.

Pay attention to how you move your body. There has to be no rolling of the eyes since it expresses disrespect. When you communicate, your focus should be on your companion. Avoid showing that you are closed off to their thoughts and emotions by not folding your arms or crossing your knees. Sit or stand at the same level as your partner; during an argument, neither party should be gazing down or up at the other.

Learn to De-escalate: When the argument begins becoming hot, it is up to you to bring things back down to a more reasonable level. The following are some sentences that are helpful in de-escalating any situation:

What suppose we were to..."

"I am aware that this is difficult..."

"I understand what you're trying to express..."

"What are your thoughts on this?"

Having an argument with your significant other is not always a terrible thing.

Dr. Gottman has said that he is a firm believer in the ability of debate to assist couples in improving their relationship. This belief is based on the many years that he has spent researching conflict. According to him, the fact that we talk about our disagreements gives our partnership "genuine lasting strength." You simply need to make sure that you start things off in the appropriate way so that the conversation might be beneficial rather than destructive.

Chapter 11

How to have a better Relationship

In this chapter , we will explore how to have a better relationship, we will see new thoughts and actions that would make us better.

Are you able to recognize a healthy relationship? A number of behaviors can predict whether a couple is on solid ground or headed for troubled waters. Of course, nobody knows what really goes on between any two people, but decades of scientific research into love, sex, and relationships have taught us that certain behaviors can tell us whether or not a couple is headed for trouble. It takes time and effort to cultivate healthy connections. They need dedication, a willingness to compromise, forgiveness, and most of all, work on your part. Continue reading for the most up-to-date information on the scientific study of relationships, as well as some engaging quizzes and practical advice that may assist you in developing a closer connection with your current spouse.

The simple part is falling in love with one another. The issue for couples is figuring out how to reignite the flames of passion on a regular basis while also cultivating the type of mature, trustworthy love that is the defining characteristic of a long-lasting relationship.

--------- *What Kind of Romance Do You Prefer?*

What exactly do you mean when you tell someone "I love you"?

We have found that the loves we experience in our most significant relationships fall into one of six main categories.

Passion and sexual desire are the driving forces behind a romantic relationship.

A feeling of warmth and profound fondness for one's best friends

logical: sentiments that are founded on common ideals, financial objectives, religion, etc. Logical feelings are practical feelings.

Feelings that are elicited by flirting or the experience of being challenged are said to be playful.

Possessive: Obsession and jealousy go hand in hand.

Selflessness is shown through nurturing, compassion, and sacrifice.

According to the findings of several studies, the love that we experience in the most significant relationships of our lives is often a synthesis of two or three distinct types of love. But it's very uncommon for partners in a single relationship to have quite diverse conceptions of what love means to them while being in the same partnership.

Dr. Hatkoff illustrates his point with the scenario of a man and a woman eating supper together. The husband does not seem to notice his wife's husband flirting with another patron as he converses with her about changing the oil in her automobile. The woman is dissatisfied with her spouse because he lacks jealousy. The spouse has the impression that his additional efforts are not appreciated.

In what way does this relate to romantic love? The guy and the lady have quite different conceptions of what love is. According to him, love is something that may be shown in tangible ways, such as by taking care of a person's vehicle. According to her, love is possessive, and the fact that her spouse displays jealousy is evidence that she is loved and appreciated.

When you have a better understanding of what it is that makes your spouse feel loved, it will be easier for you to resolve conflicts and bring the romance back into your relationship. You and your significant other can find out more about how you individually define love. If you know that your spouse is prone to jealousy, pay close attention to any signs that suggest another person is flirting with him or her. If your spouse has a sensible approach to love, pay attention to the myriad of subtle ways in which he or she expresses love by taking care of day-to-day responsibilities.

Reignite Romance

Some people refer to romantic love as a "natural addiction" due to the fact that it stimulates the reward center of the brain, in particular the dopamine pathways that are also stimulated by drug addiction, alcoholism, and gambling. However, those same pathways are also linked to experiences that are unique, energizing, focused, educational, motivating, and ecstatic, as well as desire. It's no surprise that falling in love can leave us feeling so energized and inspired.

But we all know that a love that is romantic and passionate can lose some of its intensity with time and (we hope) develop into a sort of devoted love that is more satisfied. Despite this, a lot of married couples wish they could recapture the excitement of their early dating days. But is it really feasible?

Researchers has discovered a solution to the problem of how to improve interpersonal relationships. What is the key? Try something new and unusual, but make it a point to do it together at the same time. Dopamine and norepinephrine are released in large quantities when the brain's reward system is activated by new experiences. These are the same brain circuits that become active when a person falls in love for the first time. Whether you embark on a white-water rafting vacation together or take a pottery class together, engaging your dopamine systems while you are together will help bring back the enthusiasm you had on your first date. Research on married couples has led to the conclusion that spouses who routinely share novel experiences report bigger increases in the satisfaction of their marriage than those partners who just exchange nice but known experiences.

Diagnose Your Passion Level

Elaine Hatfield, a professor of psychology, has hypothesized that the love we experience early on in a romantic partnership is distinct from the love we experience later on. In its early stages, love is said to be "passionate," which refers to sentiments of strong yearning for one's partner. When two people spend a significant amount of time together, they develop what's known as "companionate love," which is characterized by a profound attachment as well as strong sentiments of commitment and closeness.

On what point of the love spectrum does your relationship fall? You'll be able to get a better idea of how passionate your relationship.. When you have a better idea of where you are in the relationship, you can begin to focus on ways to infuse it with greater passion. Note that despite the fact that this scale is often used by academics who study love and relationships, the questionnaire in no way represents the last word on whether or not your partnership is healthy. Just do it for fun, and use the questions as a springboard to start a conversation about passion with your significant other. After all, one can never predict where a discussion may end up taking them.

-------------------Sex

The majority of couples find that the more sexual encounters they have, the better their relationship becomes.

How many sexual encounters do you have every week?

Let's begin with the upbeat news first. It's true what they say: married couples spend more quality time in bed than anybody else. Don't believe it? It's true that single individuals may regale you with tales of wild sexual adventures, but you should also keep in mind that they can go through extended stretches without having sexual encounters. According to a study that was conducted in March of 2017, it was determined that 15% of men and 27% of women claimed that they had not had sexual activity in the previous year. In addition, nine percent of men and eighteen percent of women report that they have not had sexual activity in the last five years. The greatest risk factors for living a life devoid of sexual activity include becoming older and never getting married. It doesn't matter whether you have committed or married sex once a week, once a month, or only six times a year; the simple reality of the matter is that there is someone else out there who has less sex than you do. And here's some good news for you if you're one of those individuals who don't engage in sexual activity: research shows that Americans who don't engage in sexual activity report the same level of happiness as their sexually active peers.

But Who's Keeping Count?

Even though the majority of individuals want to keep their sexual life private, quite an amount of information about people's sexual habits is public knowledge. The data come from a variety of sources, such as the General Social Survey and the International Social Survey Programme, which are studies that collect information on behavior in their respective countries, as well as additional studies from people who study sex, such as the well-known Kinsey Institute. Both of these surveys collect information on behavior in the United States. A recent study found that the sexual activity of millennials is on the decline, and the probable reason for this is that they are less likely than younger generations to have committed romantic relationships.

First and often

Having a lot of sexual encounters early on in a relationship is one of the greatest methods to ensure that your sexual life will remain vigorous throughout the course of a long-term partnership. It was found in a study conducted by the University of Georgia that more than 90,000 women from 19 different countries in Asia, Africa, and the Americas were interviewed for the study. The study found that the longer a couple is married, the less often they have sex, but that the decline appears to be relative to how much sex they were having when they first coupled up. When comparing the first year of marriage to the tenth year of marriage, here is a look at the frequency of having sex while married.'

Why does sexual activity decrease after being married?

It might be a problem with their health, the fact that they have children, boredom, or discontent in their current relationship, to name a few of the potential causes. Age is, nevertheless, a significant consideration. According to the findings of one research, sexual activity decreases at a rate of 3.2% each year beyond the age of 25. The good news is that married couples make up for any deficiencies in number with their superior quality of life. According to the findings of the National Health and Social Life Survey, married couples report having more satisfying sex experiences than single persons do.

The Relationship Without Sexual Contact

Why do some relationships seem to have more staying power than others? Researchers in the field of social science are looking for answers to the question of why some romantic partnerships end in divorce by examining no-sex marriages.

It is believed that between ten and fifteen percent of married couples had not engaged in sexual activity with their partner over the previous six months to one year. Some couples that never had sexual relations began off with very little sexual activity. Others who are in sexless marriages point to childbirth or an affair as the catalysts for the decline and final cessation of sexual activity. Those who don't have frequent sexual encounters with their spouse or committed partner tend to report lower levels of happiness and are more likely to have entertained the idea of ending their marriage than those who do.

The visit to the doctor is the first and most crucial step to take if you are in a marriage in which there is little or no sexual activity. It is possible for a person to have a low sex drive due to a medical condition (such as low testosterone levels, erectile dysfunction, menopause, or depression), as a side effect of a medicine or therapy, or as a combination of the two. Some researchers believe that the increased use of antidepressants such as Prozac and Paxil, which may reduce a person's desire to engage in sexual activity, may be one factor behind the rise in sexless marriages.

Even while there are some happy couples who are in sexless marriages, the general rule is that the more sexual encounters a couple has, the happier they are together overall. It is not simple to reignite sexual intimacy in a marriage that has been dormant for years, but it is possible to do so. Visit a physician, speak to a therapist, and start having conversations with your spouse if you want to be married but are unable to tolerate the absence of sexual intimacy in your relationship.

The following is a list of some of the measures that I propose doing in order to bring a sexually inactive marriage back into the bedroom:

Discuss the things that you both want with one another.

Have some laughs together and introduce each other to new things to do so that you can remember why you fell in love.

Hold hands. Touch. Hug.

You should have sexual encounters even if you don't want to. Many couples have found that if they force themselves to have sexual activity, it eventually stops feeling like effort, and they are able to recall that they like having sexual encounters. The body reacts by unleashing a wave of brain chemicals and undergoing a number of additional changes that are beneficial.

Keep in mind that there is no one answer to the question of how much sexual activity there should be in a marriage. The ideal quantity of sexual activity is the amount that leaves both lovers feeling satisfied and satisfied.

------A Remedy for a Happier and Healthier Sexual Life

If your sexual life has become less active, it may take some time and work to restore it back to where you want it to be. The ideal answer is one that is straightforward, but one that many couples find to be quite challenging: Begin by discussing sexual matters.

Just get it done: Have sexual encounters, even if you're not feeling very sexual. Because having sexual activity causes the body to release hormones and other chemicals, even if you are not in the mood to have it, there is a good probability that you will be very soon after you begin.

Make time for sex: It's common for partners who are always on the go to claim that they don't have time for sexual activity, but it's noteworthy to note that even the busiest individuals still manage to have extramarital relationships. The truth is that having sexual intercourse is healthy for your relationship. Put it at the top of your list.

Talk: Inquire about the desires of your significant other. Surprisingly, this seems to be the greatest obstacle that couples must overcome in order to restart their sexual life together.

The first two recommendations are self-explanatory, but let's take some time to investigate the third step, which is to discuss sexual matters with your spouse. One of the first proponents of connection science was Dr. Hatfield, who worked at the University of Hawaii. She created the Passionate Love scale that this book discussed earlier on. When Dr. Hatfield conducted a series of interviews with men and women about their sexual desires, she discovered that men and women have much more in common than they realize; however, they tend not to talk about sex with each other. The reason for this is that men and women tend not to discuss sex with each other. An easy exercise that is based on the findings of Dr. Hatfield that might have a significant influence on your sexual life is the following:

Locate two sheets of paper and two writing implements.

Now, take a seat with your partner so that each of you can jot down five aspects of your sexual encounters with your spouse that you would want to see more of. The responses shouldn't be specific sex acts (but it's acceptable to include them if that's something that's important to you). Your responses, ideally, should center on the kinds of behaviors that you would want to see more of in yourself, such as being conversational, passionate, sensitive, experimental, or adventurous.

Keep the Spark Alive here are some recommendations for how you might keep the spark alive in your relationship.

Don't stop being kind.

Are you kind and giving to your significant other? How frequently do you show that someone you care for them? Or how about doing something simple for your lover, like bringing them coffee in the morning? M en and women who score the highest on the generosity scale are much more likely to report having "extremely happy" marriages.

Make your relationship a tool for your own personal development.

To have a successful long-term relationship, one of the most crucial factors is to choose a partner that can provide variety and excitement to your life.

Here is a bit of question I have prepared in chapter one. You can go back to chapter one if you missed that . How big of a contribution has your relationship with your spouse made to the growth of your knowledge and skills? How much does your relationship with your spouse contribute to the person that you are today?

If your spouse is making you a better person, you will feel happier and more fulfilled in the relationship as a whole.

Take a Stand

The degree of care and deliberation with which a couple approaches decision-making could have a long-term impact on the quality of their love relationships. Couples who are proactive in defining their relationships, moving in together, and making wedding plans before getting married tend to have more successful marriages than couples who just let inertia to carry them through significant life changes.

"Making choices and talking things through with partners is vital." "When you make a choice after giving it some thought, you increase the likelihood that you will stick to it,"

The conclusion would seem to be self-evident, but the unfortunate truth is that many married couples postpone making decisions that really matter to them. For example, many couples who live together have never taken the time to sit down and have a conversation about cohabitation. In many cases, one partner had began spending more time at the other's house, or a lease had expired, which forced the pair to formalize a living arrangement. In other cases, the couple had already been living together informally.

To increase the overall quality of a marriage, it could be helpful to demonstrate purpose in some way, whether that be by arranging the first date, moving in together, getting married, or something else entirely. Read more on the research that went into "The Decisive Marriage" if you're interested in learning more.

---------- know who they are and what they are about" and to "make choices when it matters" rather than "letting things slip." "At the individual level, know who you are and what you are about." "Once you are a couple, in terms of how you handle important adjustments in your relationship, do the same thing you did before."

Foster relationships with family and friends.

Sometimes a couple will become so preoccupied with their connection that they will neglect to put effort into their other connections, such as those with their friends and family. M arried couples have less relationships to their extended family members than single people do. They are less likely to see family members in person, phone them, or provide assistance, and they are also less likely to engage with friends and neighbors.

The issue with this approach is that it throws an unreasonable responsibility and pressure on the relationship. W e often overload marriage by expecting our spouse to fulfill more wants than any one human can reasonably provide." And if our marriage were to fail, we wouldn't have many other sources of emotional support to fall back on.

This requires reaching out to other members of the family as well as friends on occasion for the purpose of obtaining emotional support. Encourage your spouse to maintain connections outside of the marriage and take advantage of the time apart from each other to take a break from the pressures of marriage.

See a romantic comedy.

Even though it may seem absurd, there are some evidence to show that seeing a sentimental Hollywood film about relationships might really assist real-life couples in solving their conflicts.

Having a conversation about a movie is not going to cure the major issues that are plaguing your marriage, but the results do highlight the significance of communication within a marriage and the need of seeking out chances to have conversations about your differences. According to Ronald D. Rogge, an assistant professor of psychology at the University of Rochester and the study's primary author, "A movie is a nonthreatening method to get the discussion started." This was one of the findings of the research.

The ideal movies to watch in order to get a productive conversation going are the ones that depict a relationship going through its ups and downs at different points. Several more films, such as "Couples Retreat," "Date Night," "Love and Other Drugs," and "She's Having a Baby," were analyzed as part of the research. Stay away from films like "Sleepless in Seattle" and "When Harry Met Sally" that portray couples as if they were perfect.

Epilogue

Relationships aren't easy, but far too many couples give up on theirs too soon, only to find themselves in another relationship where they engage in the same destructive habits that led to their previous breakup.

Every love relationship goes through its ups and downs, and maintaining one requires effort, devotion, and the ability to be flexible and adaptable with one's partner. But regardless of where you are in the development of your relationship or how long you have been together, there are actions that can be taken to establish a healthy connection between the two of you. You can find ways to stay connected, find fulfillment, and enjoy happiness that lasts even if you've had a lot of failed relationships in the past or if you've struggled in the past to rekindle the fires of romance in your current relationship. If you put in the effort, you can find ways to enjoy lasting happiness.

People come together for a wide variety of reasons, each of which contributes to the formation of a unique connection. Sharing a similar objective for precisely what you want the relationship to be and where you want it to go is one of the characteristics that helps to define a good relationship. You won't know the answer to that question until you have in-depth and open conversations with your spouse.

However, there are also certain qualities that are shared by the majority of relationships that are in a healthy state. It can be helpful to maintain your relationship interesting, satisfying, and exciting no matter what objectives you are working towards or what obstacles you are experiencing together if you are familiar with these fundamental ideas.

Whether you've been together for 50 days or 50 years, the fact is that the majority of relationships have the potential to be healthy and successful over the long term if both partners are willing to put in the effort to make it so.

Apply these principles above and see your relationship growing healthy in no time.

www.ingramcontent.com/pod-product-compliance
Lightning Source LLC
LaVergne TN
LVHW080557160826
845677LV00010B/1879

* 9 7 9 8 8 4 6 3 1 6 4 5 4 *